T.S. CHERRY

Let Us Make Man(Book 4)

Watchman

First published by T.S. Cherry 2020

Copyright © 2020 by T.S. Cherry

All rights reserved. No part of this publication may be reproduced, stored or transmitted in any form or by any means, electronic, mechanical, photocopying, recording, scanning, or otherwise without written permission from the publisher. It is illegal to copy this book, post it to a website, or distribute it by any other means without permission.

T.S. Cherry asserts the moral right to be identified as the author of this work.

First edition

This book was professionally typeset on Reedsy. Find out more at reedsy.com

Contents

Preface   v

I   Part One

1   About the Series   3
2   INTRODUCTION   5
3   OUTSIDE THE GATES OF HEAVEN   7
4   AT THE GATE CALLED BEAUTIFUL   10

II   Part Two

5   SECRETS OF DARKNESS   15
6   WATCHMAN   18
7   BE A WATCHMAN   21

III   Part Three

8   A TEMPORARY HOUSE   27
9   FORSEE AND PLAN   29

IV   Part Four

10	PASSOVER REHERSAL	39
11	KEEPING THE YEAST OUT OF OUR HOMES!	52
12	BRINGING DOWN THE DARK GIANT	58
13	Conclusion	61
	About the Author	65
	Also by T.S. Cherry	66

Preface

Belteshazzar, that was the dream that I, King Nebuchadnezzar, had. Now tell me what it means, for none of the wise men of my kingdom can do so. But you can tell me because the spirit of the holy gods is in you. Daniel 4:18, NLT

To fully understand this study, it is important to read the full text in the fourth chapter of Daniel from verses 10 through 26.

Daniel's interpretation of Nebuchadnezzar's dream gives us insight into ancient teachings that trees represented a kingdom or a nation. In ancient times, nations were described as trees, and we are all connected and live our lives as trees, sometimes identified by our country or sometimes identified by our spiritual lives.

Trees in modern times might be countries like China, Israel, or Egypt, which could be a spiritual community classification. China might be a tree that we know as "General jack fruit" because of how large the tree is. Israel might be known as the "Olive tree" because of the hardship the land has endured. Egypt may have been known as the "Sycamore tree".

Trees in ancient times, when books like the Torah were written, were common symbols used in the ancient world. The tree of life was one of the most popular symbols of even ancient Egypt symbolizing knowledge of the Divine plan or that equivalent to the plan of destiny.

Now, this study is a spiritual journey that will stir up your spirit. But you need to be humble enough to learn something new or be ready to think differently. To quote an avatar movie, "It is hard to fill a cup that is already full." It was hard for Christ to teach people who thought they knew the way of heaven already.

So, you must empty your cup of what you think and feel, to embark on this spiritual journey.

MAJESTY

'This is what the dream means, Your Majesty, and what the Most High has declared will happen to my lord the king. 25 You will be driven from human society, and you will live in the fields with the wild animals. You will eat grass like a cow, and you will be drenched with the dew of heaven. Seven periods of time will pass while you live this way, until you learn that the Most High rules over the kingdoms of the world and gives them to anyone he chooses. 26 But the stump and roots of the tree were left in the ground. This means that you will receive your kingdom back again when you have learned that heaven rules. Daniel 4:24-26, NLT

I like to begin by looking at the term "majesty," because often in the Body of Faith, the idea of being a king and a kingdom has a different meaning than it does from the meaning in this text.

Think about the President of the United States and his position, which is also a military position. When he retires from that position, he will maintain whatever his highest rank was, which would be the President. As a matter of fact, people always maintain the highest rank when they retire from the military. If you retire as a Captain or a Sergeant, you are addressed in the same way afterwards.

My husband is still called Captain Cherry even though he no longer holds the position or have the power and authority as a Captain. He will always be addressed as Captain because that's the last position he held before retirement.

Now, many Christians still carry the title of majesty even when they have moved out of the position of power and authority. In other words, we have a job but we haven't been given the position that we want yet. We have a business but we don't know how to take that business to the next level. We are not slaves but we are not yet in a position of power either. We have made some progress but we have digressed too.

It means, we look better on the outside but Satan is attacking our emotions and basically running our lives. We have declared the kingship and blessings but they haven't manifested in our lives.

If that describes your life, then this is for you. I want you to know that you are the tree in the midst of the garden. This message changed my perspective of things and I'm hoping that it would bless you as well.

The Dream and the Garden

I was doing some study of the Book of Daniel and I realized that Daniel's interpretation of Nebuchadnezzar's dream sounded like the tree in the Garden of Eden. I decided to do a deeper study also of the Book of Genesis. I realize that the beginning of Genesis reads very much like a dream. It occurred to me that perhaps, Nebuchadnezzar was asking for the meaning of Genesis.

What is the meaning behind the tree of life and the two trees that are in the Garden - the tree of good and evil? What are their purposes? What does this mean? Or, how does it apply to my life?

Daniel goes on a mission to try to explain this to Nebuchadnezzar. And if you begin to see it that way, you realize it opens up a whole new thought pattern that can be applied to your personal as well as your business life. This book is focused on how we must re-examine the secrets of darkness and the ancient understanding of the Sons of Man who were chosen to be " Watchman".

I want you to know that you are the tree in the midst of the Garden. You have the title but you need to move into the fulfillment of the promises of God. This is book 4 in the " YOU ARE THAT TREE" as the sons of man learn to become the Tree of Life; this series is focused on the watchman a key element that must be learned before you enter the gates of heaven. In modern ideas, we might describe this as entering the promised land and beginning our journey as Abraham. In this book, we are at the gates of heaven.

Part One

As much as you see and appreciate 'the light,' you need to know also about 'the darkness' and its potential effects on your life. This understanding will help your preparedness and make you ready to face whatever comes. That way, you'll never combat an ensuing problem with the wrong approach

1

About the Series

Hi! John here – and on behalf of T.S Cherry and her team, I'd like to share with you exciting news about her latest series, "Let Us Make Man: An Expose on the Seven Heavens".

That are four recently released books from the series of 12 books that describe the Ancient meaning of MAN, as it follows Man as the tree of life and his journey from the First to the Seventh Heaven.

There has already been much excitement surrounding her first book which has become a best-selling first installment, "You Are That Tree: The Garden of Eden", which has reached #1 on Amazon.com. The first book, an expose on the two trees in the Garden of Eden, teaches us about differentiating the voice of the snake from the voice of God. Removing obstacles in our way to self-discovery and enlightenment.

The much-anticipated sequel's meanwhile talks about the 'seven basic steps' that represent the pattern for the healing of life, marriage, business, family, and your community.

It explores the process of discovering your purpose; being an entrepreneur, creating a sub-culture that is self-efficient, extracting ancient wisdom, and exploring the sciences and knowledge of Ancient Egypt, Isreal, and other ancient civilizations to regain lost knowledge that is relevant to current times.

Grab a copy of the sequel books and unravel the secret to your life's healing!

2

INTRODUCTION

Put Watchman at the Gate – Watchman - is the fourth in the series, LET US MAKE MAN. This volume is beautifully divided into four parts:

Part one stresses why you need to know about 'darkness' and its potential effects on your life just as much as you see and appreciate 'the light.' It explains that it's very necessary to be taught about the light, but if the plan of the enemy is left uncovered, he can take you out because you were not prepared against him. And the reality is that you have to prepare against the enemy. But to do that, you need to have the secrets of darkness.

Part two is a direct sequel to part one, and explains how the secrets of darkness are monitored by "Watchmen". It expounds on the importance of spiritual alertness in the hour we are. It's easy to be distracted by several happenings around. But you'd rather want to stay alert than be taken unawares by unlikely events orchestrated by 'darkness.'

You'll learn that God never instructs us to assign watchmen when trouble comes, but long before trouble surfaces. Beyond that, He wants us to become watchmen for our communities and churches. In this part, you'll come to understand how to align yourself with peak physical, spiritual, mental, and financial preparedness in times like this.

Part three explains the best way you can function in the office of the watchman – by building huts or providing temporary solutions. You will learn that the whole world looks up to you – the watchman - for the solution they need. And though you may not be able to provide a permanent solution, you can provide a temporary one right where you are.

You'll study the basic differences between watchmen and gate-keepers, and why the enemies were often after the knowledge that made a nation great. You'll also learn how to possibly spare the people around you from unnecessary unpleasant surprises.

Part four is the bonus content for this volume and provides Scriptural wisdom to survive contemporary times. It unfolds the season when you can probably get to understand the difference between man's solutions and God's solutions.

So far, we can say that our lack of knowledge has destroyed a lot of people, including those dear to our hearts. But this is something that we have the power to overcome; something that we have the power to change. That is what this book is all about. You'll find it an invaluable companion IN TIMES LIKE THIS!

3

OUTSIDE THE GATES OF HEAVEN

Genesis 1:1-3 says, "In the beginning, God created the Heaven and the earth. And the earth was without form and void; and darkness was upon the face of the deep. And the Spirit of God moved upon the face of the waters. And God said, Let there be light: and there was light."

Darkness can be defined as those things that put us in bondage. That includes everything from our philosophies to our experiences. It finds its strength mostly in our senses - what we think, what we feel, what we see, and what we're taught. All these help put chains on our minds, and move us further and further away from God's purpose for our lives.

As much as we see and appreciate the light, we need to know also about darkness and its potential effects on our lives. Such understanding can help our preparedness and make us ready to face whatever comes. The lack of this understanding can result in trying to combat an ensuing problem with the wrong approach.

Some time ago, we traveled from Virginia, which is surrounded by water, all the way to El Paso, Texas. My daughter was just about three months old. She began to have this skin disease, and I took her to the military posts. They had a hospital there.

I took her there about five or six times on posts for an additional three months. At this point, she was about six months old. Within these three months, her skin was getting progressively worse.

At six months, the skin over her face was covered with some dry scales, and it looked horrible. She was crying and scratching at it and the doctors could not help her.

I finally decided to take her to someone local, a Mexican doctor. The military, of course, would not pay for it because it didn't go through their system. This doctor, of course, was a local doctor and not within their system. So, I had to pay the $100 to see him.

This doctor took just one look at my daughter, and in about five minutes, he was able to say what the problem was. He gave her a particular cream that cleared the skin disease in three days.

This doctor could not even speak English. We spoke through an interpreter. Yet, he was able to solve in five minutes what I had been back and forth with the military doctors for about three months.

What was the problem here?

Very simple; wrong medication. If someone has asthma and is given medications for high blood pressure, the tendency of asthma not going away is high.

So, the persistence of my daughter's skin disease was due largely to the inability of the military doctors to prescribe the right medication for the problem, and I have learned valuable lessons from this.

This is the same thing that happens spiritually. If you are prescribed the wrong medication for your spiritual needs, you will definitely run into serious trouble. If you need spiritual counsel for your marriage, business, etc., but get the wrong prescription, you might – like my daughter – suffer longer for something that could be solved in a moment.

You see, the doctor - for instance - who writes your medical prescription, may have a degree from medical college. Nevertheless, if he is not qualified to handle your health problem and writes the wrong prescription, you can suffer longer.

I'm using this analogy to help you understand the problem when you have the wrong person give you advice on a matter, or when you have a wrong teacher in your life. This was the problem of some people in Bible days, and this is the problem with many in the church today. The teachings either leave you blind or lame, which leaves you outside of the gates of heaven. Mark says it this way.

> ***Mark 7:13, NIV*** *"Thus you nullify the word of God by your tradition that you have handed down. And you do many things like that."*

4

AT THE GATE CALLED BEAUTIFUL

Acts 3:1-7 says, "Now Peter and John went up together into the temple at the hour of prayer, being the ninth hour. And a certain man lame from his mother's womb was carried, whom they laid daily at the gate of the temple which is called Beautiful, to ask alms of them that entered into the temple; Who seeing Peter and John about to go into the temple asked an alms. And Peter, fastening his eyes upon him with John, said, Look on us. And he gave heed unto them, expecting to receive something of them. Then Peter said, Silver and gold have I none; but such as I have give I thee: In the name of Jesus Christ of Nazareth rise up and walk. And he took him by the right hand, and lifted him up: and immediately his feet and ankle bones received strength."

You've probably heard or read the story of the lame man at the gate called Beautiful. It is so frustrating that this man was at the gate but not able to get in. I can say that he suffered from a problem of 'wrong prescription.'

Now, a lame man is not blind. So, the problem he's having is not with the secrets of light but the secrets of darkness. Thus, darkness is holding him back through lameness or diseased feet. He doesn't know how to get rid of the darkness in his life, so he's living with it.

In other words, the doctors who are at the synagogue are prescribing him medication, but it's not healing his lameness.

Here's the problem: the synagogue is focused on the light. And while they're focused on the light without teaching the secrets of darkness, the people's darkness is creating half of their problems.

You see, I have to teach you about the light, yes, but if I don't cover the plan of the enemy, when he comes, he will take you out because you are not prepared against him. The reality of it is, you have to prepare against the enemy. And to do that, you need to have the secrets of darkness.

When people don't prepare for the darkness ahead, they put themselves at a disadvantage because when it comes, things happen that make them think God has forgotten them. And it's not that God has forgotten them, but that the teachers have left them lame at the gate.

They gave them the secrets of the light but failed to give them the secrets of darkness. And without the secrets of darkness, they only have half the story. We do understand that the light is the life of man, yes, but we also have to understand what's coming.

Darkness is the plan of the enemy and the Lord often reveals that plan to us ahead of time. Why? Because He wants us to recognize the plan of the enemy and know what to do when it comes.

We must understand that darkness can plunder when we don't have the secrets. This is what we see in the life of the man at the Beautiful Gate. Basically, he's been at the gate his whole life, and darkness has been running his life for a very long time.

Just like my daughter's case, what should have taken a few days essentially took him most of his life because he just didn't have the secrets of darkness. It wasn't being taught to him properly. He was taught about the light but not darkness. In other words, he was being taught a one-sided story.

My question to you today is, where are you?

Are you already at the gate but can't enter in to partake or take possession of what God has prepared for your life?

Are you going round in circles with the same problem without finding a way out?

Are you struggling with the wrong prescription over the challenges of life?

Think about your business life.

Do you have all the secrets of light for your business?

Can you clearly see the obstacles ahead? Can you see the darkness head-on?

What about the relationships in your life?

Do you see why God sent the people in your life that He sent?

Do you see the light and darkness in the people in your life?

Perhaps the people you thought you could trust, you can't; and the people you thought you couldn't trust are the people you actually can depend on.

To move ahead meaningfully with your life, you need to understand the secrets of the light and the secrets of darkness. A balance between the two will help you rise from wherever you are or whatever has crumbled you and gain access to God's place or position for your life.

II

Part Two

You need to understand the secrets of the light and the secrets of darkness. The secrets of darkness are monitored by "Watchman". You certainly want to stay alert, prepared, and ready at all times. You don't want your life, health, business, etc., taken unawares by any unlikely events orchestrated by darkness. Secrets of Darkness will help you understand how to align yourself with peak physical, spiritual, mental, and financial preparedness.

5

SECRETS OF DARKNESS

We are in a season of darkness one of the most critical seasons in the history of our lives and nation.

1 Corinthians 4:5 Therefore judge nothing before the appointed time; wait until the Lord comes. He will bring to light what is hidden in darkness and will expose the motives of the heart. At that time each will receive their praise from God. (NIV)

It is important to note the darkness does not necessarily mean a season that the devil rules. It can also mean a season of judgment.

1 Corinthians 11:31 But if we were more discerning with regard to ourselves, we would not come under such judgment. (NIV)

However, no matter if we are in a season of darkness because of our enemies or because of our own doing. It is certain that it is time for us to return to God as a nation and as individuals.

Some people believe that there should not be a mix of politics with the Bible. But the reality of it is, if politics affects your daily life and God affects your daily life, then you're making the wrong separation.

How can we desire God's protection but don't want to involve Him in our lives and the happenings in our nation? If we want God's protection, we have to involve Him in everything - our life, health, business, political system, etc.

We must get back to God and lay before Him in utter surrender until His mercy intervenes in the situation of our world; until we get instructions from Him on the way forward.

As we lay before God to get instructions, the Bible gives us some ideas on what we should do.

Ezekiel 33:1-6 says,

1 And the word of the LORD came to me, saying,

2 Son of man, speak to the sons of your people and say to them, 'If I bring a sword upon a land, and the people of the land take one man from among them and make him their **watchman**,

3 and he sees the sword coming upon the land and blows on the trumpet and warns the people,

4 then he who hears the sound of the trumpet and does not take warning, and a sword comes and takes him away, his blood will be on his own head.

5 'He heard the sound of the trumpet but did not take warning; his blood will be on himself. But had he taken warning, he would have delivered his life.

6 'But if the watchman sees the sword coming and does not blow the trumpet and the people are not warned, and a sword comes and takes a person from them, he is taken away in his iniquity; but his blood I will require from the watchman's hand.'"

In times like this, God wants us to assign watchmen. Interestingly enough, He doesn't say that we are to assign watchmen when trouble comes. But rather that we are supposed to have watchmen long before trouble surfaces.

More than that, God also wants us to become watchmen for our communities and churches.

But who is a watchman? What is his role? How does he influence the happenings around people?

Answers to these questions, and much more, are what you're about to encounter here. You will come to understand how to align yourself with peak physical, spiritual, mental, and financial preparedness in times like this.

6

WATCHMAN

Who is a Watchman?
There is a magazine I get so often. It is called The Trends Journal. One of the things this Journal does is to look at trends in the economy by looking at previous trends. So basically, it studies trends, and almost like science, comes up with predictions for the future.

It deals with economies and investments, and the direction of society: everything from gold to what stocks people should buy per time. That helps economies and people to decide what companies to buy, and what companies not to buy.

A watchman is almost like someone who reports things in the line of The Trends Journal. He warns people ahead of time. He tells them how to prepare ahead. He helps people keep in step with things that are going on by providing them with adequate information.

He gives information about things that apply to the life, health, business, etc., of the people. He gets information on all levels to help the people prepare ahead.

So, I want you to think of a watchman as a lookout; and not just a lookout but a well-informed lookout that spends days, nights, and even the Sabbaths trying to interpret what goes on per time.

In essence, he is the one that helps prepare the people for what is coming.

Set Up Watchmen

One of the most important things that God sets up is essentially the defense of His people. So, He tells His people to set up watchmen.

The Biblical perspective of a watchman is someone who looks out for swords or anything that might attack his people - whether economically, spiritually, or politically. That's why watchmen are also called watchdogs.

God wants us to have people who are watchmen for our communities and churches; people who have collective information. One person may have one piece of the puzzle, and somewhere else another may have another piece of the puzzle. When put together, there's a whole picture of what to watch out for.

Now, rather than simply providing people with the news of what is happening or about to happen, a watchman gives instructions on how they can find protection.

So, for instance, more than just giving the news that oil prices have gone to zero, a watchman tells the people what to do to save their finances from unwarranted losses.

In essence, the watchman's job is to let the people know what is happening and give them strategies and potential ways in which they can protect themselves.

In Biblical terms, he is to sound the alarm and warn the people ahead of time. But more than that, he is to tell them what to do to handle what is to come. He does not simply bring news but proffers solutions or recommendations based on ongoing trends.

Now, it is important to state that a watchman's recommendations are based on real information, not just emotions, feelings, or thoughts. He provides information based on a revelation from God and based on scientific, or other relevant evidence. The watchman might say that based on their prayer they believe that the next world destruction could be fire; using scientific evidence they might say that we believe the last destruction was not a flood of water but ice. (The ice age) Now, we expect the temperatures of global warming to rising to the point that fire consumes not just Florida over the next 50 years but, other states as well, making it impossible for life to survive without a plan of action. Our plan is to begin to build underground. Based on ancient evidence of the ant people and The Derinkuyu **underground city** (Cappadocian Greek: π Malakopi) which is an ancient multi-level **underground city** in the Derinkuyu district in Nevşehir Province, **Turkey**, extending to a depth of approximately 60 meters (200 ft). **The Ant People** not only **survived** the cataclysms but had a safe harbor in prepared **caves** and great stores of food.

7

BE A WATCHMAN

Ezekiel 33:7 says, "Now as for you, son of man, I have appointed you a watchman for the house of Israel; so you will hear a message from My mouth and give them warning from Me."

This is not something to be taken lightly. This is something that can affect a person's livelihood. It is something you want to be mindful of. God says He is appointing you a watchman, and all the explanations I have given in the previous chapter is your job description.

Essentially, you are to hear from God at all times about what's next. God hands down something and you sound the alarm to warn the people.

From the foregoing, it is easy to see that the job of a watchman requires you to know and understand the modes of God's appointment. And that includes understanding the seasons, feasts, etc., which are nothing more than dress rehearsals to help you recognize when to sound the alarm.

Some people may pay attention to what you say, others may not. But you must see that the people are warned ahead of time. It is like the commercial that says, "Take this medicine but the side effects are this and that."

That's more like what you do as the watchman. You say, "Hey, the government has said that they're trying Pepcid AC, but if you have this or that underlying health condition, you may have an issue with it."

Or, you may be saying something like, "One of the things they're seeing over in China is that young people in their twenties or thirties are having blood clots. So, be mindful. And if you already have issues with clotting, bring that to the attention of your doctor. If you feel any symptoms of Covid-19, be in constant communication with your doctor."

Again, the president, some time ago said something like, "You may be able to take some kind of disinfectant as an injection."

Now, you want to make sure you completely clear that up with your people; that you **cannot** take household disinfectant to help with Covid-19.

You want your people to know that we do not use bleach within our bodies. We do not inhale it. We do not take baths in it. Those are things we don't do. So you have to put that information out, and make sure that your people understand that this is neither safe nor deemed appropriate.

That's what God wants you to do; to be a watchman for your community and church. And I am saying to you, "Sound the alarm! Be the watchman for your people!"

A Hearty Prayer

I wish to end this by saying that we send out prayers to our Rabbis and the Pastors of different assemblies as they handle the destruction that the Coronavirus has had on us, taking our brothers and sisters home earlier than we would have wanted them to go home.

We also send out our prayers to the Ministers in our different communities who are thinking of things they can do. We pray that God gives them clarity and direction, so that they may understand what is coming forth and what needs to be done in this hour.

"O Lord, we need Your Bread today. Yesterday's bread won't solve today's problems. We need the bread for today. We need the Manna for today, so that we can get instructions for our daily life. Guide and water our footsteps, clear our mind and erase any obstacles that could hinder us from seeing the solutions that are readily in front of us. Lord, we ask that you take away the blindness, and heal our eyes for such a time as this, so we know that you are the Lord, in Jesus' Name we pray."

AMEN!

III

Part Three

A Temporary House is a sequel to Sound the Alarm, in the Watchman series. Watchmen build huts, a temporary dwelling for a temporary situation. You are the watchman the whole world looks up to for the solution they need. You may not be able to provide a permanent solution, but you can provide a temporary one for the temporary situation upon us right now.

8

A TEMPORARY HOUSE

Job 27:18 says, "He builds his house like a spider's web, Like a (temporary) hut which a watchman makes" (AMP). One of the things watchmen make is a hut, which represents a temporary solution.

As I mentioned in an earlier chapter, it is the watchmen's job to let the people know what's going on with the secret (darkness). It is their job to inform others. They are, essentially, the first go-to people.

To effectively be a watchman, there is a need to understand more about ancient watchmen.

In ancient times, people built cities to protect themselves from invading armies. When the watchmen spotted a coming threat, they would sound the alarm and all the people that were outside of the city would run inside, and the city gates would be shut. That way, the people were protected.

Sometimes, I think people confuse watchmen with gatekeepers.

The watchmen were the first line of defense. They protected the people. The gatekeepers, on the other hand, protected the sacred knowledge. That knowledge was not limited to the Torah. It included their science and inventions; information that made the country great.

That knowledge was what the enemies were often after - the knowledge that made the nation great. That is why they would often attack and get such information, then take all they wanted and burn the rest to the ground.

So, while it was the duty of the gatekeepers to make sure the sacred knowledge didn't fall into the wrong hands, it was the duty of the watchmen to make sure the people were protected from danger.

The question now is, how would people's life change if they had you as their watchman? How would you help to spare them unnecessary unpleasant surprises? That is what you are about to learn here.

9

FORSEE AND PLAN

> Ezekiel 33:6
> But if the watchman see the sword come, and blow not the trumpet, and the people be not warned; if the sword come, and take [any] person from among them, he is taken away in his iniquity; but his blood will I require at the watchman's hand.

Think about it, if you had information ahead of time about a happening, what would you do differently?

What would you do differently if you knew something wrong was coming?

If you had a heads up that you were going to lose your job; or you had a heads up that the enemy was coming to destroy your family; what would you do differently?

If, for example, you knew seven years earlier, that there was a coming pandemic, what would you plan for? What would you get? What would you stack?

You know, sometimes when you get a warning, as a watchman, you think you have more time. But the truth is, you often don't. So, when you get the notice, you have to plan the best way you can and make provision that covers everything.

You have to compile a list and vet it with other watchmen to provide something that the people of God can utilize and plan effectively.

This is exactly what I did.

I didn't have a date when it would surface but I knew the pandemic was coming. I gave that information to some people that I cared about. I shared it with a close friend about six years ago.

When the pandemic happened, one of my oldest friends called me. She went out and got everything she needed because she remembered what I had told her. She said, because of what I told her, she emptied her bank account and got the necessary things. That's because she already got news of what was coming.

So, more than just the understanding that something is coming, as a watchman, you must draw up a plan of action and make a preparation list of what is essential.

It is your job to foresee, but beyond that, you should draw up a plan of action. You are not like the news anchor that just delivers the news. You have to offer some kind of solution - even if it isn't a hundred percent. You have to offer something. That is your job. You are solution-oriented.

Speak it Out!

Think about what advantage you would have over the enemy if you knew what he was planning.

God's kingdom is designed to help you plan against unwarranted attacks of the enemy; and not just the attack of your enemy, but the attack of someone who claims to love you - the attack of your friends, essentially.

I want you to understand that when it comes to attacks, you need to defend yourself by speaking out what you have inside of you. But you must have something inside before you can speak it out. You cannot speak out peace if you don't have peace. You cannot speak love if you don't have love.

Now, you must speak out what God has deposited inside of you, and not just what you feel.

The most important thing for you to understand as a watchman is the difference between your emotions - what you feel - and what the Spirit of God is leading you to say or do. That way, you won't get emotionally involved in a situation and hand out your personal opinion.

Your personal opinion is important, yes. But it's more important that you line up with what God has to say, and that you speak out what He has deposited within you.

If God gives you a spirit of peace, then speak out peace. If God says there is an attack in the night, then let the people know. If God is saying that the sword is coming, then tell the people the sword is coming.

You must be in tune with the Spirit of God. Your words and mood must be based on the Spirit of God at each moment and season.

Peace Be Still!

To help you understand what I'm trying to pass across, I'll share a personal experience of something that happened some time ago.

I was in the house when the wind started blowing extremely

strong. When I looked out the window, I couldn't even see directly in front of me. It was so windy that you could put your hands out and not see your hands. That's how bad it was.

I told my children and my husband to start praying and then all of a sudden, I felt a spirit of calmness. I should have been scared because there was a whistling sound, almost like a train on the tracks. I thought it was a tornado. And because of how strong it was, I realized it had to be directly over us.

Yet at that moment I felt an overwhelming spirit of peace that just wasn't normal for the situation. I quickly concluded that the Lord was protecting us. Of course, I should have or normally would feel overwhelmed, but I didn't. And when you experience something that is not normal for a situation, you know that God is in it.

As I began to pray, I felt God's peace. I mean I was just overcome with it. So I said, "I speak peace to this storm."

Instantly, the storm was calm.

I was a little nervous because it got so calm I wondered if I was in the eye of the storm. I've often heard that in the eye of the storm, it is extremely calm.

I was concerned because it went from something like a tornado to the utmost calm. You can imagine, just a moment ago, you were scared to go outside because you could get blown away. Then suddenly, you couldn't hear anything.

About fifteen to twenty minutes later, we went outside the yard and found hail everywhere. I realized that the storm had done some damage to houses around but we had no damage. I lost some fruit from my tree, but that wasn't any real damage.

Here's the point about this: I had to speak what was inside of me. And that's what you must do. You must speak out of what God puts in you. When you get that feeling inside, speak it out.

If you feel peace, speak peace.

Understand the Difference

You see, a watchman's job is to understand the difference between the Spirit of God and what's normal for the situation. Yes, you do have things that are normal that you can deliver to the people of God, but you are supposed to be sensitive to the Spirit of God and speak what He says for the situation at hand.

Think about what would happen if I didn't speak out. What if I didn't even have the understanding to speak out what was within me? My house could have been damaged like the neighbors' houses or worse.

We need to be able to understand this so that we don't perish needlessly like the disciples on the boat almost did. During the storm, they didn't understand that someone had to speak a word of peace to the storm.

All they needed was "Peace be still," but they knew nothing about it. You see, a lot comes from understanding what is required in the hour and situation we find ourselves.

What you'll garner from all this is that if you are prepared for what is coming, it gives you peace in the storm and gives peace to those around you because they also get prepared. They feel the love of God through you. Essentially, you become the extension of God so that they feel that love.

The question now is, what Word has God placed within you that needs to be spoken over the current situation that's going on right now?

Until the Oil Flows

The oil – the anointing - is important in times like these. We must understand that we don't move until the oil flows. We don't move until we find the person that has the anointing for the situation.

Many have spoken but until the one whom God gives authority to speak in this hour speaks it out, we are going to have a problem.

Now, the oil can flow on the least, or from the top. Think about David. He was considered the least. He was the last person people would ever think could take down Goliath.

What that means is that you don't underestimate yourself or the people that surround you. And that's important because sometimes you have a contribution to make. Even if you feel like it's meaningless. Even if you only have the power to calm a small storm, that's important. It can help out.

In the same vein, seek out the people you don't think have anything to contribute. You may be surprised at what they can offer.

Pay Attention to your Dreams

A watchman's job is to understand what comes next. And as a watchman, you may have to pay attention to your dreams because sometimes they do have more meaning than you think they do.

If you don't understand them, you may want to write them down and get back there over and over and over again until you can get more information and clarity.

Watchmen should always, always, always write down their dream, no matter how crazy it is because it could be that God is trying to say something.

We want to know the secrets of the light. That's important, but we also need to know the secrets of darkness. Dreams are a really good source of getting information concerning darkness.

I have noticed that a lot of times when the Lord wants to tell me something about the plan that the enemy has, He does so through my dreams. So, we need to be mindful of that.

Finally

Now the question is, as a watchman, do you know what next to plan for? Are you getting information from God? Or, are you just waiting on the world to tell you how to respond to what's going on?

It's time to wake up!

Romans 8:19 tells us that "the earnest expectation of the creature waiteth for the manifestation of the sons of God." In other words, the world, the whole world is waiting on you to become the solution they need. You may not be able to provide a permanent solution at the moment, but you can provide a temporary one.

Job 27:18 says, "He builds his house like a spider's web, Like a (temporary) hut which a watchman makes." (AMP)

A hut is simply a temporary dwelling for a temporary situation. That's what you should be building right now - a temporary house; a temporary solution for a temporary situation that is upon us right now.

That is your job as a watchman.

IV

Part Four

Bonus Secrets of the Night this is " WATCHMAN"
Content based on current times.

Isaiah 21:6

For thus hath the Lord said unto me, Go, set a watchman, let him declare what he seeth.

Kings-2 9:17

And there stood a watchman on the tower in Jezreel, and he spied the company of Jehu as he came, and said, I see a company. And Joram said, Take an horseman, and send to meet them, and let him say, [Is it] peace?

10

PASSOVER REHERSAL

Ezekiel 3:17
Son of man, I have made thee a watchman unto the house of Israel: therefore hear the word at my mouth, and give them warning from me.

It is good to take a quick look at the times we're in right now. I'm sure that some of the things I have already written about are beginning to unfold.

Beloved, this is the moment to be able to access God in a way that you've never been able to access Him. This is the moment to be able to get information from God that you may not even have thought to access before.

Now, you'll ask the hard questions that perhaps you wouldn't have asked before. This is the season when God is most active; the season when God has answers for you. This is when God shows you Who He is. This is when you get to understand the difference between man's solutions and God's solutions.

A Significant Passover

Now, we're living in the time of the Passover, and people are trying to understand the Passover like never before.

We've been told the children's version of these stories for so long, but the practical aspect of what's going on is not often taught in our churches and synagogues. So, the reasons behind what we do for Passover sometimes has left us. Consequently, we find that we're deep into the observances without adequate knowledge of why.

It's like the story of the woman who cuts off the ends of the ham before getting it fried. Then her two daughters, who saw her do it, also fry the ham the same way she does by cutting off the ends. When asked why they did it that way, the daughters had no explanation but only to say it was the way their mother did it. It had become a tradition for the family.

When they decided to go back and ask their mum why she prepared the ham that way, she explained that she did it because the ham didn't fit in her little pan at that time. Her daughters had a bigger pan and could change that tradition, but they didn't because they didn't even know in the first place, why it was done.

In other words, they had a pan that was big enough for their hams to go in and didn't need to cut off the sap. But you see, if you don't know the original reason why some things were done, you just keep on repeating them needlessly.

We see a lot of this in the Passover season.

Living Sacrifice

Let us take a look at the primary purpose of the Passover.

I'll veer off a little and talk about the familiar story of Cain and Abel.

Both Cain and Abel brought an offering of their choice to the

Lord. Cain offered something he grew from the ground. He wanted to create his way to God, which was the same problem that existed later on at the Tower of Babel when the people wanted to find their way to God.

On the other hand, we know that Abel stayed steadfast to what he was taught. He observed the requirements of God, which was to live off the Word, and not just the Word, but every Word that proceeded out of the Mouth of God. He offered a living sacrifice. And if we're honest, that is essentially the Passover story.

Now, like Abel, when we're creating our Passover meal, what we are essentially doing is, we are offering our sacrifice. We are saying that we're not going to be like Egypt, we're not going to offer that which grew from the ground because we have learned better, and are teaching our children better, too.

At least, we now understand that even though we are eating the lamb as a living sacrifice, we are supposed to be the living sacrifice.

A Better Understanding

We should have an overall understanding that God is essentially Lord over our lives and that we are meant to submit to His decisions over ours, even when we don't understand. So the lamb in the Passover is simply a picture of our being able to lay down our lives as a sacrifice from generation to generation.

When you look at it from the point of utmost surrender, you see that God wants more than just your Sunday morning. He wants every second, every minute, and every day of your life. He wants the way you interact with other people. He wants the way you do business. He wants the way you give medical treatments. He wants the way you build your communities. He wants all of that so that He can guide or direct you.

God wants you to walk with the Holy Spirit so that you can have a compass. He wants to shade some light into your life, so you don't try to navigate your way in the dark. And that's where we see the difference between Cain and Abel.

Abel had seen the light. He knew there was a better way. It may not have been in his culture, but he was exposed to the light and had come to a better understanding.

Cain hadn't seen the light. He was still offering up the same things he had always offered. He wasn't spiritually enlightened. Beyond that, he hated his brother for seeing the light and having a better understanding than he did.

Today, we see 'Cain and Abel' play out before us daily: religion versus light; man's ideas versus God's enlightenment; problems versus real solutions.

Baal: A Different Teaching

If you look at it critically, both Cain and Abel were taught essentially by the same person – their mother. And the truth is, mothers have to be the primary teachers of their children, and not television, environment, or culture. Mothers must teach their children to navigate this world like Cain and Abel's mother taught them.

But you see, despite their mother's teaching, Cain chose to go his way. He chose a path different from what he was taught. He offered up to God whatever he wanted, but Abel followed the right path.

In Cain's jealousy, he went ahead and murdered Abel. Nevertheless, when you look at the descendants of Abel and that of Cain, you see a major difference. One is the progenitor of a religion that has God at the center of it while the other is a progenitor of a religion of the East.

This is important!

Both religions originated from the same place. The difference is how they interpret the information they have. It is not that one has a better Bible than the other. It's simple! They have the same Bible; the difference is how they interpret it.

Baal was a god worshipped in many ancient Middle Eastern communities, especially among the Canaanites. Baal is not a Hebrew word. Its origin is semantic. The word in its original translation means "husband." And you know, the curse on the woman was that she would submit under her "husband."

This would mean that her punishment was to submit to the religion or culture, which was Baal. And Baal is, of course, an interpretation or manipulation of, not just God's Word but His understanding and solutions. It's just a different way of teaching.

That was Eve's punishment.

So, we see that when she gives birth, half of her lineage submits to God and the other half submits to Baal, which represents the ways of the world. It's like raising two children, and one child is saved while the other child is not. Essentially, that's what Eve experienced.

Getting the Leaven Out

We understand that the Passover is about the lamb, and it's about making sure that we are offering a living sacrifice. But there's also one primary thing that is important and is done all the way up into the day of Passover. That is getting the leaven out of the house.

There are always spiritual as well as practical applications. The spiritual application is that yeast represents sin. We want to get sin out of our homes.

The practical application, on the other hand, is that yeast in the body breeds disease. In other words, the more you like to eat bread, the more grounds the disease has to grow and feed within you.

It has been proven that a sick body is more acidic. And in acidic environments, yeast essentially grows faster. In times like these, it is both recommended and advisable that we abstain from yeast, and I have written extensively on this in another article I'll love you to read (please find the link here).

For this time and period, I am restraining from bread; call it a fast if you will. But my Passover agenda is to refrain from bread and to try and get my body to be as alkaline as possible.

This is what I believe some people did in the Spanish Flu: They took one tablespoon of baking soda every day to make the body more alkaline. I take a bath with bombs which are made mainly of baking soda daily, without citric acid.

Keep Fear Out!

Another thing you must constantly do is to keep fear out. You don't want the enemy to use this as an advantage. You need to be one step ahead of him and put your fears aside. This is a time where you need to lay on your face, seek God, and be responsible.

David said, "Though I walk through the valley of the shadow of death, I shall fear no evil." In the world, fears become 'yeast.' Thus, you must remove all fear from your body, by resisting whatever science tells you, that causes fear.

Keep fear out!

A Real Battle

Sometimes we fail to measure darkness by its impact on us and those around us. But sooner or later, darkness always lets us know it is there. It tries to secure a home in our fear, in our tiredness, in our inability to measure its presence. The World of Darkness is just as real as the world of light and they are both fighting for the place of being Lord over us.

Invisible enemies have one thing in common: They study you while you fail to study them. So, with every attack, the enemy evolves and gets better at what he does. Make no mistakes beloved; light and darkness are very real.

The Bible tells us many secrets about the lord of darkness and his desire to rule. There are certain environments where darkness thrives. You know, sometimes we call cancer darkness, but it is not limited to cancer. It takes pride in getting you to eat certain kinds of food. These cravings affect your pH balance, and when that happens, the body becomes more susceptible to diseases.

Just as I've already pointed out, the Torah teaches us that during the Passover, we are to get all the yeast out of our home. In like manner, we are to get all yeast out of our body. If you go through these teachings without realizing that yeast brings disease, you can be negatively impacted.

Like cancer, yeast grows and you feed it the same way you feed bread - with flour and sugar. So, the Torah is telling us to get all the yeast out of our bodies, and the things that feed it - sugar and flour.

Light and Darkness

Our lack of knowledge has destroyed a lot of people. But this is something that we have the power to overcome; something that we have the power to change.

In Judaism, darkness and light are considered two different realms or two different worlds. But the Bible makes it abundantly clear that God reveals the secrets of darkness. So, if you understand that darkness has secrets, it means that God can reveal to you the darkness behind the disease.

God can reveal to you the things you need to do to help you get through this disease. He can reveal to you the plans of the enemy, even an invisible one. He can help you plan practical things that you can do, like growing seeds, using baking soda as a way to make your body more alkaline, etc.

The truth, beloved, is that in your darkest hour, you need light.

Come Out on the Other Side

I will never forget when I was grieving for my son and I went to a pastor. He was recommended because he had lost a child. But I realized he hadn't the light. He couldn't help me. He had experienced it, but he hadn't come out on the other side.

Now, there is something important about going through it and seeing the light. That helps you understand that sometimes life happens and sometimes we lose people. In such cases, how do we get through our grief?

Grief is such a dark place. It goes through the fiber of who we are and makes us question everything we thought we knew; every experience we thought we had.

Grief will tear one side of you from the other. It is one of the few things that does not care who you are. Grief affects the highest as well as the lowest person.

Well, whether it is the loss of a child you loved or the loss of your identity, God wants you to see a new light, and come out on the other side. But how do you know you have seen the light? By proffering or providing solutions.

If you look at the majority of inventions and the solutions that have come to the world, even in horrific times, many of them admit that God gave it to them. And if you pay a bit of attention, you will discover that the Jews, who have practically gone through a lot, have quite a greater number of scientific inventions.

The Jewish people have made such enormous contributions to Science, Medicine, Economics, etc., that the secular world cannot claim ignorance. The truth is, that's the way God sends solutions. He sends it through people being able to create solutions that have never been created before.

So then, it's not just about being able to pray your way through your circumstance; it's about seeing the light and being able to create solutions. It's about being able to go get your brother. It's about being able to feed people; it's about being able to help people; it's about being able to save lives.

Balance it with Prayer

As much as there are things you can do to help give you a powerful body, you must also find a balance between them and prayer. Think about the battle between Israel and the Amalekites. For as long as Moses the man of God kept his hands up, Israel would win. But when his hands came down, Amalek would begin to gain power over Israel.

So, it was more like, if the man of God stopped praying, they would lose the battle. That was because it was not simply a one-sided battle. It was a blend of doing what needed to be done spiritually while fighting physically.

That's the way it is with us today. No matter how much we can do to stay healthy and resist infections, there must be a balance of prayer to keep us on the victory side. 50% of doing what needs to be done in prayer, and 50% of doing what needs to be done nutritionally and medically, get us there.

You must understand how to address things in the natural - the medications you should take, putting on the mask, getting the yeast out of your house, etc. These are natural things that you can do. Then, align yourself with the power of prayer. You can't do one without the other, both are needed to be able to handle the secret of darkness.

Thinking Differently

Think for a moment on the scenario in John's Gospel about the man who was born blind. The disciples of Jesus wanted to know if it was the fault of his mother or father. Jesus said it was none of those, but that God would be glorified.

Today we are in a situation where blindness has covered the earth, and we're busy trying to find out, "Who is responsible for this?" It is not necessarily the mothers or the fathers who raised us. Rather, God allowed this! That's all Christ is saying. God has allowed it for such a time as this so that when He takes the blinders off, you will be able to see the difference between God and the systems of the world.

In times like these, rather than concern ourselves with who's at fault or who's not, we need to begin to think differently. We may not be able to congregate as a church but we can still be connected.

As pastors, for instance, we must be able to give our people some practical things to help ease their fears. Get into holistic health. Talk about controlled breathing if they're having trouble breathing. Talk about making sure that they have their face mask on at all times. Let people have important information because it saves lives.

A lot of communities are running short of food, and some farmers say they have stuff in the fields going bad. This is the time to get together with the farmers and say, hey, can we put on our mask and come pick the food that you have out in the fields going bad? We can pick the food and distribute it to the people at our church through the drive-through lines.

You can speak to some restaurant owners who have a drive-through, and find out if you can utilize their drive-through to be able to hand out goods to certain people. You can partner with some people and get these things done. It's just a matter of seeing what's available, looking at the problem smartly, and finding solutions.

That is what Christ is about. Christ is about bringing light into the problem. Light is the solution. It is the ability to help, and find a way. It is not about putting people at risk; that is selfish. It is about finding out if people are safe. It is about taking time out to check if they have their medications.

I love what one particular community did. They blocked off the village and got some persons who go out to get everything they need, then bring it to everybody. That's a good solution. You should also identify and do some problem solving using practical approaches that can help in your neighborhood.

Begin to look two, three, four months down the road. Prepare your people. Get seeds together. There are some companies right now that are only selling to farmers. Get those seeds and plant them. Also, give some seeds to other people to plant. And it can be just as simple as giving them a seed that's planted in a self-watering pot and dropping it off on their front porch. That could be tomatoes, cucumbers, etc.

A self-watering pot is just a matter of two buckets with a plastic cup in the middle and a piece of PVC pipe. If you go to the store it might cost you $30, but if you make it yourself, it'll cost you $2. So, for $2 and some cents, you can grow the tomato seeds by putting them in cups, so that when the time comes, you could be able to hand out tomato and cucumber plants, so that people can have fresh vegetables.

Think about it, your health depends on being able to have access to fresh foods. I know you have some canned foods, but you do need fresh produce.

Recognize the Light

If the world has a problem, you have to look around because darkness does not take God by surprise. Somewhere, God has already created a solution, which is the understanding of darkness and discovering the light.

Isaiah 45:2-3 says, "I will go before you,...and level the mountains. I will smash down gates of bronze and cut through bars of iron. And I will give you treasures hidden in the darkness—secret riches. I will do this so you may know that I am the Lord, the God of Israel, the one who calls you by name." At this time, a lot of people are displaced. So, you must think of different things that you can do, probably a little different from the norm.

I heard a story about people who were in the 9/11 towers. There was a lady who was in charge, and she said to others, "We are going up to the roof." She was the team leader and the people were following her. But one young man said, "No, I've seen this before. We go down, and go out." He said, "I'm not going up; I'm going down."

Going up was protocol. The protocol called for them to go to the roof and wait for an airplane to come and rescue them. But he knew when to break off from what protocol called for. He was able to survive, and those who followed him were able to survive. That was because he took a different route. He followed a different path from what had been previously outlined.

It was protocol. It was what was put in place. It was the best information they had about how to survive if there ever was an attack. But that information was wrong. And many times amid the moment, you need somebody that knows when the given information is wrong. You need to know when to follow protocol and go up to the roof to wait for an airplane or when to break protocol and walk away. Everyone that followed the young man, lived. But everyone that followed the leader, died.

That is a very, very hard lesson to learn. They only had moments to make that decision. And sometimes that's all we ever get when the time comes. You only get one chance to decide either to follow protocol or break from protocol. That's all you get. It's a powerful lesson. It's a lesson that some people have to learn the hard way.

I see a world of darkness, but in the darkness, God is saying, "Let there be light." However, the thing is, you need to recognize the light amid the darkness because it won't always come from where you think it should come. It may not come through who you think it should come, or the method you think it should come.

The light may not always come through religion. Sometimes it will come through science. But it may not always come through science. Sometimes it will come through religion. Yes, that is the truth. Sometimes it will come through schools, too. But whichever way it comes, you must have the flexibility to be able to recognize the light that's in the darkness. That is what is going to save you, in times like these.

11

KEEPING THE YEAST OUT OF OUR HOMES!

Ezekiel 33:2, KJV
Son of man, speak to the children of thy people, and say unto them, When I bring the sword upon a land, if the people of the land take a man of their coasts, and set him for their watchman:

While we try to grapple with the situation at hand, I'd love to share a bit on something I think is very important for each person to consider, and that is Keeping the Yeast Out of the House.

On the last day of Passover, I thought deeply about a few things; and this year's Passover was like none other. The current plague has shade light on our tradition and caused us to experience Christ in a new way. A lot of things have changed for me, and I was able to bring them to the modern-day context, but I'd love to focus particularly on yeast and hyssop.

Speaking about the Passover, Exodus 12:14-15 (NIV) says, "This is a day you are to commemorate; for the generations to come you shall celebrate it as a festival to the Lord — a lasting ordinance. **For seven days you are to eat bread made without yeast. On the first day remove the yeast from your houses,...**"

Now, I'll like you to pay attention to the sentences in bold for a while.

First, it says, "...you are to eat bread made without yeast." This is very significant for a time like this. And it doesn't just have to be limited to bread but also aged cheese, mushrooms, yeast-processed and cured meats, dried fruits, gravy, and stock cubes, processed fruit juices, vinegar containing ingredients, alcohol (brewer's yeast), etc.

Why is God's command on what I'll call "yeast abstinence" important for us at this time? Well, it will interest you to know that yeast is a potential harbor of viruses. A paper by Richard Yuqi Zhao of the Institute of Human Virology, University of Maryland School of Medicine, Baltimore, explains that some yeasts are natural hosts for viruses. Many positive sense (+) RNA viruses and some DNA viruses replicate with various levels in yeasts.

You can see with me that the Bible is right!

I am aware that America tends to consume large amounts of yeast, but you can refrain from eating bread and other high yeast products at this time. The truth is, you lose nothing by doing a "yeast fast," that is, keep yeast out of your body for some time. That sacrifice is simple for most of us to do.

The second thing that Exodus 12:14-15 says is that you are to "...remove the yeast from your houses,..." So, God is saying to clean your house and make sure that there is no yeast or diseases found there. The emphasis here is eliminating the disease-causing agents from your house, and there are many ways to do this.

I have heard, for instance, that the virus can be trapped on the bottom of your feet. So, if you leave your shoes off at the door, there is the possibility that it does not get into your house. And if you have a wooden floor and other such surfaces, they are very easy to sterilize, wipe down and clean off.

You will also find that the best environment for yeasts to grow is also the best environment for disease to grow - that is in dark, dirty and damp places. So, you may need to open the windows and also wipe things clean, so that the disease does not have a comfortable place to thrive.

You see! The biblical "keep the yeast out of your house" can have a very practical application in this season.

Pray and Keep Positive

Keeping the yeast out of your home is not just about cleaning the house but also cleaning your mind. You must equally keep the yeast out of your mind, by praying and keeping positive so that your negative thoughts do not have grounds to breed.

In times like this, you must focus on the positive. Maybe you have to post positive stickers or notes from faith-building Scriptures or listen to God's Word over and over. But do whatever you need to do to keep your mind focused on the positive.

Yes, I know you want to be aware of what's going on, pay attention to the news, and keep up with what is happening. You may be mindful of the news, but you should not allow it to control your emotions.

A lot of times, to keep positive, I pray and play praise and worship music in my house. I mostly turn it on loud, so that the music can be heard all through the house. That way, there is a positive atmosphere in the house that keeps all the negativities away.

Avoid Grief

Listen, this is for many of us tough times, but you must do your best to avoid grief. I need you to understand that grief weakens the immune system, and can put you in danger.

If you know a little about my story or read it in any of my books, then you probably have heard about my son's death and the lessons that I learned at that moment. If I had succumbed to grief, I wouldn't be here today.

In this time where I have lost loved ones, I have to be very mindful. Probably the time will come to grieve, but that time is not now. Sometimes, certain things like a video that my family sends around tend to trigger something, but I catch and guard myself because I understand that now is not the time to grieve. Instead, I keep my mind focused like a soldier in the war front. I put my grief away until my life is no longer in danger.

Hyssop Helps

The final thing I want to discuss here is the idea of hyssop in the Bible. I'm sure you are familiar with the word 'hyssop' at least if not anywhere else, in Psalms 51:7 where David prayed, "Purge me with hyssop, and I shall be clean;"

Hyssop is an interesting choice as a cleansing agent. It is an herb that grows just under three feet in height, producing clusters of variously colored flowers. The short, cut stems of the plant can be gathered into bunches, and in the Old Testament, these bunches were used for several purposes.

Exodus 12:21-22 (NLT) says, "Then Moses called all the elders of Israel together and said to them, "Go, pick out a lamb or young goat for each of your families, and slaughter the Passover animal. Drain the blood into a basin. Then take a bundle of hyssop branches and dip it into the blood. Brush the hyssop across the top and sides of the doorframes of your houses. And no one may go out through the door until morning."

In the above Passover event of Exodus 12, God directed that the Israelites dip a bunch of hyssop into the blood of the Passover Lamb, and sprinkle or brush on the doorposts and lintel of each home. Also, in Leviticus and Numbers, hyssop was used as part of sacrificial ceremonies. The hyssop was always tied into bunches for use in sprinkling the blood of the sacrificed animal.

Research shows that hyssop contains valuable antiseptic or cleansing properties that would "disinfect" a contaminated person or his possessions. It is said that the Romans used it because they believed it helped protect them against plagues. The herb is useful today for many health issues including, digestive and intestinal as well as respiratory problems.

It is useful for liver and gallbladder conditions, intestinal pain, and loss of appetite. It can also be used to eliminate coughs, prevent the common cold and respiratory infections, soothe sore throats, and remedy asthma.

Today we don't use hyssop for sprinkling, so you may not have it around, but you do have access to bleach. So, as you receive some supplies at your door, take some bleach, put it in a spray bottle, leave it on the front porch of your house for at least three hours and then go outside.

The virus lives in the air for about three hours, and so when someone drops something for you at the front porch, you can leave it there for about three hours, spray it out with some bleach, and then bring it into the house. That provides added protection for you and your family.

In conclusion, we can do our part of cleaning the yeast out of the house, as well as make sure that it does not grow in our thoughts and minds through grief and negative thinking. We can also put the ordinance of sprinkling with hyssop into modern-day use and provide added protection for ourselves and our loved ones in the midst of the chaos and uncertainty.

12

BRINGING DOWN THE DARK GIANT

Hosea 9:8, KJV
The watchman of Ephraim [was] with my God: [but] the prophet [is] a snare of a fowler in all his ways, [and] hatred in the house of his God.

Today the whole world is in the midst of a situation that presents so much uncertainty on every front – the coronavirus outbreak. There is a lockdown in virtually every affected country right now. Consequently, I am writing to share or bring some motivation on a few things you can do while you are on lockdown.

A lot of people are trying to hear from the heavens, and they are wondering what they are supposed to be doing right now. The Word that God has given me for today is a call to the sons of David to bring down the Goliath in their communities or wherever they find themselves.

Now, I want you to think about it. Have you ever faced a battle that you were not necessarily prepared to fight? For some reason, you felt like the little person fighting against what many would consider a giant. The enemy seemed to be more powerful and had many advantages you didn't have.

Well, the Bible tells us that such a battle came against Israel. The battle was so fierce and brought fear to the hearts of the entire army.

In the midst of that, David was sent to take food to his brothers on the battlefield. Of course, the food was a great encouragement. But he also brought encouragement to the people through the Word of God.

The Word of God he brought was more than just mere words of encouragement, it was essentially a call to action. His words became the 'Manna' if you will, that they needed to bring down the giant.

Under his leadership, and with no more than the Words of God, David was able to conquer what seemed like a battle of a lifetime against the giant. Without David, Israel would have lost that battle.

The Bible gives a similar example of the Lord Jesus saving a people that had completely lost hope in a terrible situation. The disciples of Jesus were facing a great storm. Jesus was asleep on the boat. But the disciples woke Him up and said, "Teacher don't you care if we drown?"

The Gospel of Mark tells us that Jesus woke up and immediately addressed the situation. He did not address the people but the issue. He rebuked the winds and commanded the sea to be still. In other words, He gave the solution that brought peace at that moment. The boisterous winds ceased and there was a dead calm.

Now, notice that Christ was under the title of the Son of David. When they needed Him to solve a problem, they recognized Him as the Son of David. In essence, they recognized Him as being able to access God and take away all the problematic issues by bringing a solution from heaven for the moment, just like David did for Israel.

Listen, your community needs you to be that son of David in this global pandemic. That is what the community needs right now. There is a giant that is attacking them, and they need you to help them bring him down. There is a storm that is blowing against them, and they need you to calm that storm and bring the peace that is above all understanding.

They just want you to offer a solution. It doesn't matter whether that solution is to feed the hungry or make phone calls and ensure that everyone in the church has the provisions they need. That is essentially the peace that you need to bring to the people right now.

I want you to think very carefully about the coronavirus and understand something. If God allowed us a level of attack, then it is obvious that He will also send that same level of solution.

You need to be that solution that people need at this time. You must be ready to convert what you have into what other people need. Whatever God has laid on your heart to do, pray about it, fast on it and seek God's guidance on it.

Rather than recline into worrying, take this time to look towards the future and rethink your business model. As you may know, some people are already turning restaurants into grocery stores, just to provide what is needed.

In this moment, evolution is key! Your ability to think, and come up with solutions for your family, business, community and the church is very vital and most needed. So, be the son of David in every possible way you can in this season.

Remain blessed.

13

Conclusion

*He replied, "The knowledge of the **mysteries of the kingdom of God** has been given to you, but to others I speak in parables, so that, 'Though seeing, they may not see; though hearing, they may not understand, **Luke 8:10, NIV***

In the Garden of Eden, there is a ***tree of life*** or the "tree of souls" which is designed to be the highest level of consciousness that a nation can reach united as "One". In order to enter the gates of heaven, you must overcome both **blindless**- which is understanding the secrets of the light and **lameness**- which is understanding the secrets of darkness.

Blindness: Is not having knowledge of the **mysteries** of the Kingdom of God.

Therefore judge nothing before the appointed time; wait until the Son of Man (Lord) comes. He will bring to light

> what is **hidden in darkness** and will expose the motives of the heart. At that time each will receive their praise from God.

Lameness: Is not having knowledge of what is hidden in **darkness**. Sometimes in the bible, it can be called a sword.

> But if the **watchman** sees the **sword** coming and does not blow the trumpet to warn the people and the sword comes and takes someone's life, that person's life will be taken because of their sin, but I will hold the watchman accountable for their blood.' NIV

Note:

Darkness is not limited to the plans of the enemy but it can also be the plans of God.

> *Mathew 10:33- 35*
>
> But whoever denies Me before men, I will also deny him before My Father in heaven. Do not assume that I have come to bring peace to the earth; I have not come to bring peace, but **a sword**. For I have come to turn 'a man against his father, a daughter against her mother, a daughter-in-law against her mother-in-law

Like God that has the power of both light and darkness. The Sons of Man has the ability to wheel both " light" and "Darkness". As you might have guessed, we have just scratched the surface of the secrets of the light and darkness. A watchman's journey begins by understanding the rehearsals. The Jewish holidays, feasts, and festivals that are all designed to reveal ancient secrets. The danger is allowing your light to go out, by allowing these days to become another thoughtless religious day of traditions. Here is a list of a few great places to start.

- Shabbat. The day of rest and weekly observance of God's completion of creation.
- **Rosh Hashanah**. The **Jewish New Year**—a holiday observed with festive meals and a day spent in prayer or quiet meditation.
- **Yom Kippur**. The Day of Atonement is the holiest day of the year in Judaism.
- **Sukkot**. commonly called the Feast of Tabernacles or in some translations, the Festival of Shelters, and known also as the Feast of Ingathering, is a biblical Jewish holiday celebrated on the 15th day of the seventh month
- **Shemini Atzeret**. - The **conclusion** of Sukkot, or one additional **delay** after the seven days of Sukkot.
- **Simchat Torah**. Simchat Torah or Simhat Torah is a Jewish holiday that celebrates and marks the conclusion of the annual cycle of public Torah readings, and the beginning of a new cycle.
- **Hanukkah**. Festival commemorating the rededication of the Second Temple in Jerusalem at the time of the Maccabean Revolt against the Seleucid Empire. It is also known as the Festival of Lights.
- **Tu B'Shevat**. Also called Rosh HaShanah La'Ilanot, literally 'New Year of the **Trees**'

My Final Thought I will leave you with this Torah Verse.

*Matthew 24: 42 Therefore keep watch, because you do not know the day on which your Lord will come. But understand this: If the **Master of the House** had known in which watch of the night the thief was coming, he would have kept watch and would not have let his house be broken into. For this reason, you also must be ready, because the **Son of Man** will come at an hour you do not expect.*

About the Author

Author T.S. Cherry is a Holistic Teacher and Author that focuses on herbal medicine and the spiritual healing through the 7 heavens

Also by T.S. Cherry

YOU ARE THAT TREE
STEP INTO THE NEXT LEVEL OF LIFE!

You are the Tree, an exposé on the two trees in the Garden of Eden, opens up on the power within you, either to be the tree of life - which is the expression of God through flesh - or the tree of good and evil.

The author expounds deeply on the forbidden apple, which is the "way without God; the path of self; the way of disobedience." She explains the consequences of "giving the forbidden apple a bite," which is to make a decision to follow your own path in life, instead of God's.

Learn in this blockbuster book, how you can differentiate between the voice of the snake and that of God, which is the first major struggle of many people. And, how you can put the "snakes" – the wrong voices and influences - out of the garden of your life.

This is your season to step into the next level of life!

Answers

There's never been a better time to access God than in critical moments like this. This is the season when God is most active, will show you Who He is, and has answers for you. This is when you get to understand the difference between man's solutions and God's solutions.

While we try to grapple with the situation at hand, I'd love to share a bit on something I think is very important for each person to consider, and that is Keeping the Yeast Out of the House.

On the last day of Passover, I thought deeply about a few things; and this year's Passover was like none other. The current plague has shade light on our tradition and caused us to experience Christ in a new way. A lot of things have changed for me, and I was able to bring them to the modern-day context.

BEUNIQUE MAGAZINE #01
WHOLISTIC LIFESTYLE- WRVA-107 Richmond's Wholistic Malt Shop Cafe serving up #Talkradio #holistictalkBeUnique Magazine & Radio Show Take Risks, Find Yourself, Express Yourself! offering a fresh look at the business, and brains, of unique holistic culture.

www.ingramcontent.com/pod-product-compliance
Lightning Source LLC
Chambersburg PA
CBHW052121110526
44592CB00013B/1701